MUSICAL INSTRUMENTS OF THE WORLD

Strings

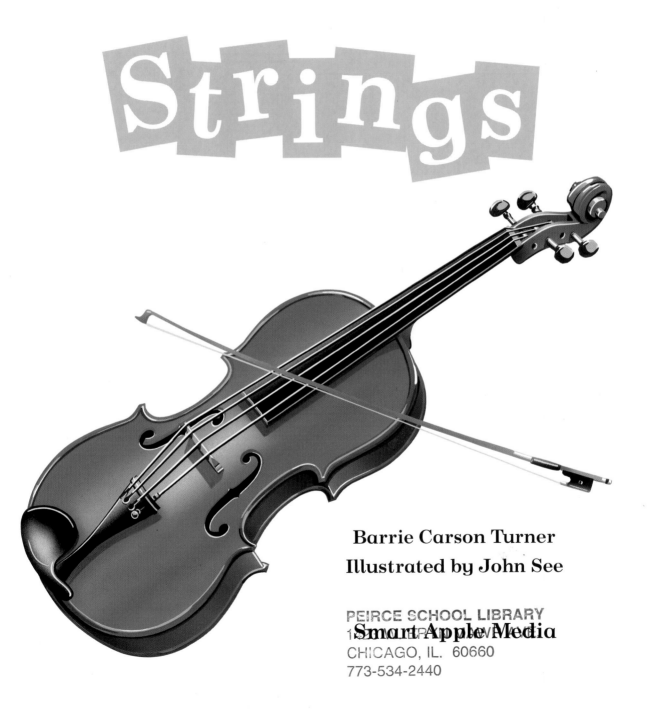

Barrie Carson Turner

Illustrated by John See

Smart Apple Media

First published in the UK in 1998 by
Belitha Press Limited
London House, Great Eastern Wharf,
Parkgate Road, London SW11 4NQ

Text by Barrie Carson Turner   Illustrations by John See
Text and illustrations copyright © Belitha Press Ltd 1998
Cover design by The Design Lab

Published in the United States by
Smart Apple Media
123 South Broad Street
Mankato, Minnesota 56001

ISBN: 1-887068-47-3

Library of Congress Cataloging-in-Publication Data

Turner, Barrie.
    Strings / Barrie Carson Turner.
        p.   cm. — (The musical instruments of the world)
    Includes index.
    Summary: Describes eighteen stringed instruments from all over the
world including the violin, mandolin, moon guitar, and koto.
    ISBN 1-887068-47-3
    1. Stringed instruments—Juvenile literature.   [1. Stringed
instruments.]   I. Title.   II. Series.
    ML460.T88 1998
    787'. 19—dc21   98-6280

Printed in Hong Kong / China

9   8   7   6   5   4   3   2   1

Picture acknowledgements: Sue Cunningham Photographic: 15;
Eye Ubiquitous: 27; Getty Images: 29; The Hutchison Library: 9, 17,
21, 23, 26; Panos Pictures: 13; Performing Arts Library: 6, 11, 12,
16, 19, 20, 25; Redferns: 4-5, 7, 22; John Walmsley Photo Library: 8.

Contents

Musical

Musical instruments are played in every country of the world. There are many thousands of different instruments of all shapes and sizes. They are often grouped into four families: strings, brass, percussion, and woodwind.

Stringed instruments make a sound when their strings vibrate. Percussion instruments are struck (hit), shaken, or scraped to make their sound. Brass and woodwind instruments are blown to make their sound.

This book is about the string family. Stringed instruments can be plucked, struck, or bowed. Most have a hollow body called a soundbox.

instruments

Some soundboxes are simple, and others are carved into beautiful shapes. For this book we have chosen 19 stringed instruments from around the world. There is a picture of each instrument and a photograph of a performer playing it. On pages 30 and 31 you will find a list of useful words to help you understand more about music.

Double bass

The double bass is the largest and lowest-sounding member of the string family. The instrument has four thick strings. The player pulls a bow across the strings to make them move. Players often pluck the strings, especially when musicians play jazz. This action adds a bounce to the music. The tallest double bass ever made is almost 17 feet (5 m) high.

tuning peg

bow

string

fingerboard

sound hole

bridge

spike

Double bass players stand up or sit on a high stool when they play.

Mandolin

tuning peg

fret

fingerboard

sound hole

bridge

strings

The mandolin was first played in Italy about 300 years ago. A mandolin is shaped like a pear and has a deep body. Mandolins are often beautifully decorated. The metal strings are plucked with a plastic plectrum. Mandolin players quickly play each note many times to make a beautiful shimmering sound.

People often play folk music on the mandolin.

Cello

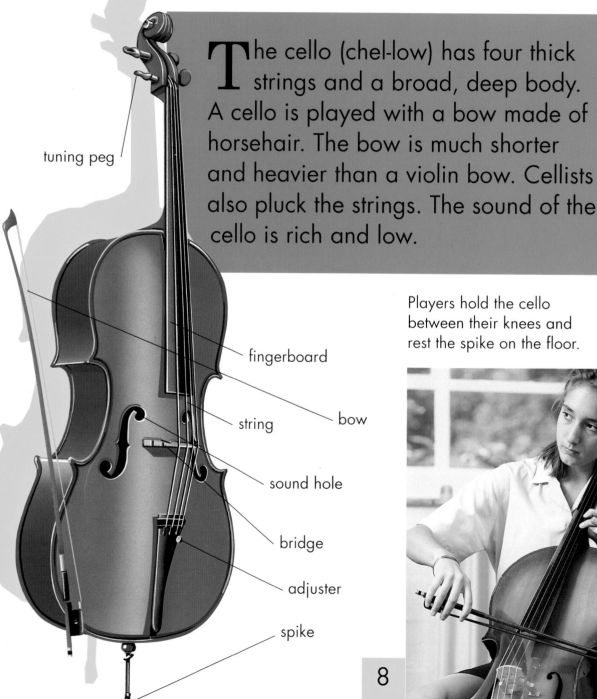

The cello (chel-low) has four thick strings and a broad, deep body. A cello is played with a bow made of horsehair. The bow is much shorter and heavier than a violin bow. Cellists also pluck the strings. The sound of the cello is rich and low.

tuning peg

fingerboard

string

bow

sound hole

bridge

adjuster

spike

Players hold the cello between their knees and rest the spike on the floor.

8

Moon guitar

The moon guitar has been played in China for more than 1,500 years. This guitar received its name because of its lovely round shape. The moon guitar has four strings which are tuned by turning the long pegs. Players use their fingers or a plectrum to pluck the strings.

The moon guitar has a quiet, delicate sound. This guitar is often used to accompany singers.

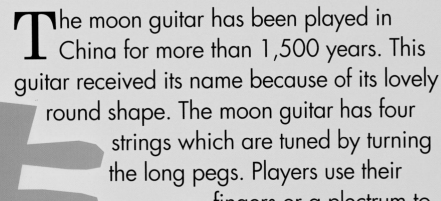

tuning peg

fret

string

bridge

Sitar

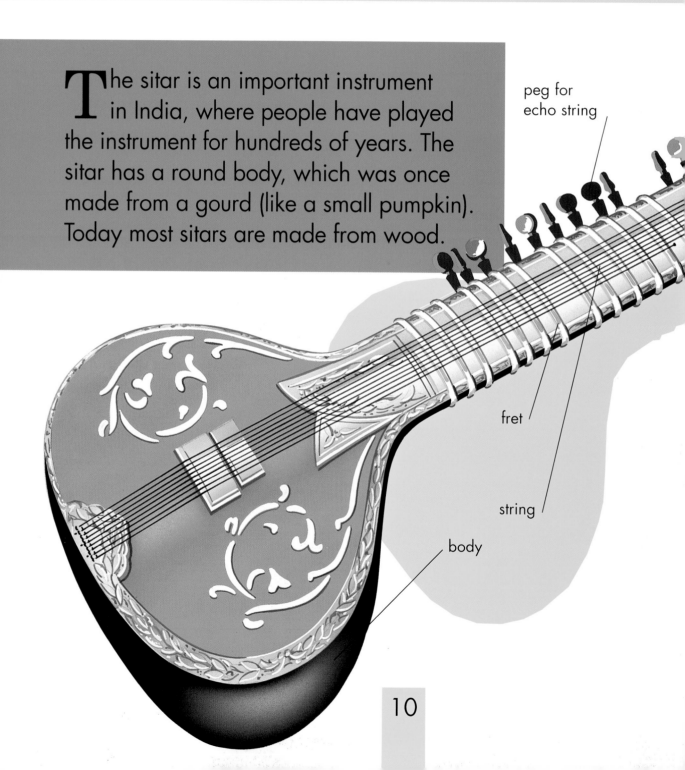

The sitar is an important instrument in India, where people have played the instrument for hundreds of years. The sitar has a round body, which was once made from a gourd (like a small pumpkin). Today most sitars are made from wood.

peg for
echo string

fret

string

body

10

neck

The sitar is plucked with a wire plectrum. The highest sounding string plays the tune. The thin bands of metal along the neck are called frets. The frets can be moved. Different fret positions make different tunes. The player pulls the string across the fret. This pulling gives the sitar its whining sound.

Sitar players only pluck the strings held by the large pegs. When they do this, the strings held by the small pegs make an echo sound.

Banjo

The banjo was brought to North America from West Africa some time around 1700. The instrument was made from a gourd cut in half, with a sheepskin tied tightly over it. Modern banjos are made from wood. The banjo has four main strings, which are played by the fingers. Another shorter string is played by the thumb.

frets

thumb string

fingerboard

belly

string

bridge

Players pluck the strings of the banjo like a guitar or sometimes brush the strings with the back of their nails.

Ukulele

The ukulele (yoo-cuh-ley-lee) has four nylon strings and looks like a small guitar. It was first played in the Hawaiian islands, and its name means "little flea." The ukulele soon became very popular because it was small, easy to play, and light to carry around.

string

fret

fingerboard

sound hole

The ukulele is plucked and strummed like a guitar. A ukulele has a bright twanging sound.

13

Cimbalom

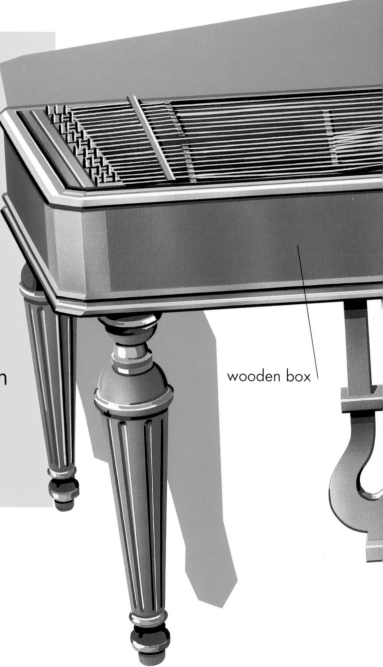

The cimbalom (chim-bal-om) comes from Hungary. The instrument looks like a large wooden box on legs. There are many strings inside the box. The player taps the strings with thin wooden or wire beaters. The beaters are covered with a soft cloth, which helps to give the instrument its warm ringing sound.

wooden box

strings

Cimbaloms have been played in Hungary for more than 400 years. The cimbalom on the left is a big, loud one. It is used for concerts. The player presses a pedal at the bottom to keep the sound of one string from mixing into the sound of the next.

The cimbalom is played as a solo instrument as well as part of a group. In Hungary the instrument is often played in restaurants, hotels, and cafés.

15

Violin

The violin has four strings and a curved body and is played with a bow. The bow is made of wood and horsehair. The violinist pulls the hair across the strings to make music. Sometimes violinists pluck the strings. Violin music can sound gentle and sweet or loud and strong.

tuning peg

fingerboard

string

bow

bridge

sound hole

adjuster

chin rest

Violinists use their fingers to press the strings on the fingerboard to make different sounds.

16

Dulcimer

tuning peg

sound hole

strings

Dulcimer (dul-si-ma) players usually rest the instrument on their knees or a table. They tap the strings with beaters made of wood or wire. They also pluck the strings with their fingers or a plectrum. Gypsies have played the dulcimer for hundreds of years throughout Europe.

beaters

bridge

soundbox

The player hits the strings gently with the curved part of the beater to make a soft ringing sound.

17

Koto

The koto is one of Japan's most famous instruments. A koto is long and narrow and rests on the ground. The instrument's curved body is made of wood. Once upon a time, the strings on a koto were made of silk. Today they are usually made of nylon. Players pluck the strings with plectrums that fit over the thumb and two fingers of the right hand. The plectrums look like small thimbles.

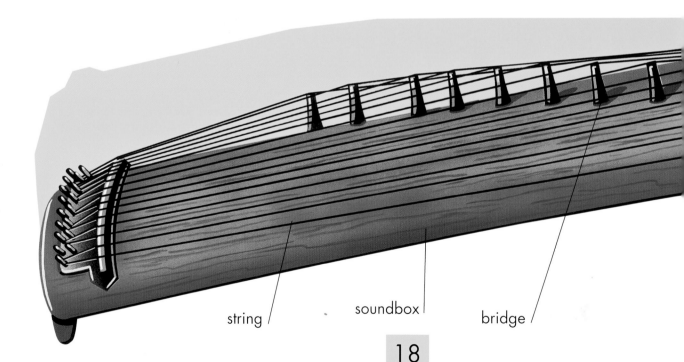

string   soundbox   bridge

In Japan, people often play the koto at home to entertain their family and friends. The koto can be played as a solo instrument or as accompaniment for other instruments and singers.

Each string has its own bridge, shaped like the letter Y but upside down. The bridges hold the strings away from the body of the instrument. This allows them to sound clearly.

Viola

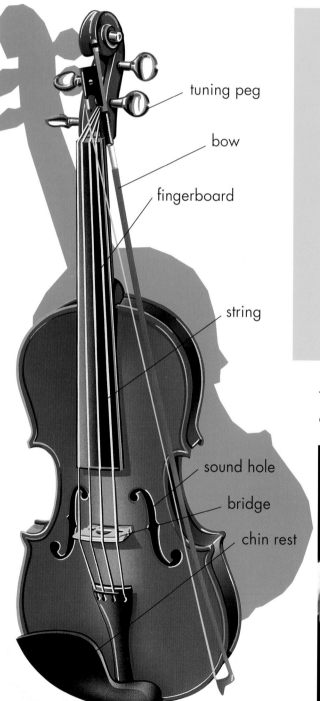

tuning peg

bow

fingerboard

string

sound hole

bridge

chin rest

The viola looks like the violin, but a viola is a bit bigger. It has four strings and is played with a bow made of horsehair. Sometimes players also pluck the strings to make music. The viola is mainly used in orchestras. Not many people play it as a solo instrument.

The sound of the viola is lower and richer than the violin's sound.

Bandura

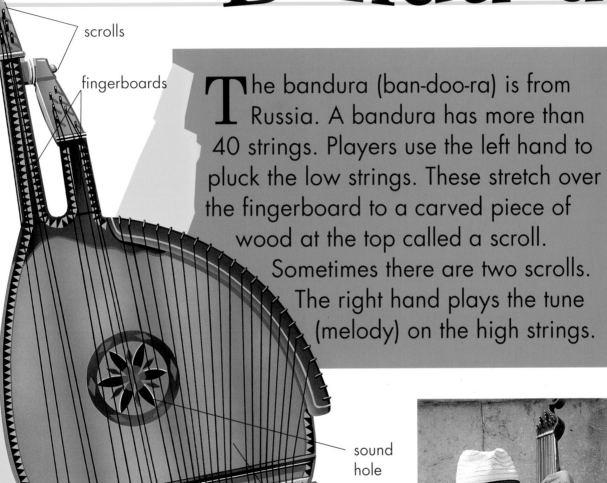

scrolls

fingerboards

The bandura (ban-doo-ra) is from Russia. A bandura has more than 40 strings. Players use the left hand to pluck the low strings. These stretch over the fingerboard to a carved piece of wood at the top called a scroll. Sometimes there are two scrolls. The right hand plays the tune (melody) on the high strings.

sound hole

high (melody) string

low string

The bandura sounds like a small harp. A bandura is played as a solo instrument and also in groups.

21

Guitar

The guitar was first played in Spain more than 400 years ago. Today the guitar is used to play pop and classical music. The fingerboard has thin strips of metal called frets, which show guitarists where to put their fingers. Guitarists can play single notes or chords. Guitar strings are plucked or strummed with the fingers or with a plectrum.

In classical music, guitarists play sitting down, with the guitar resting on one leg. Pop musicians usually play standing up.

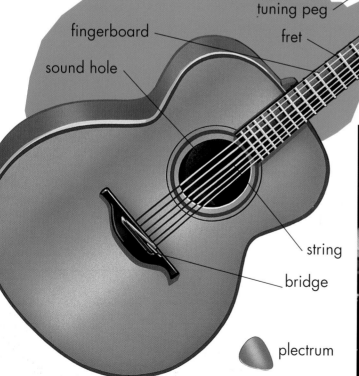

tuning peg

fingerboard

fret

sound hole

string

bridge

plectrum

Musical bow

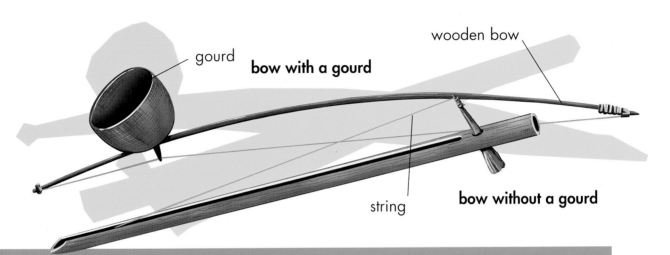

gourd

bow with a gourd

wooden bow

string

bow without a gourd

The musical bow is one of the oldest stringed instruments. The bow is shaped like a shooting bow. Musicians pluck the string, rub it with a short stick or bow, or even play the instrument with their teeth. Sometimes players attach a hollow gourd, or even a tin can, to the stick to make the instrument louder.

The musical bow is played in many parts of the world. Musicians sing as they play. They also accompany singers and other instruments.

23

Harp

The first harps were played thousands of years ago. Today there are harps in many shapes and sizes all over the world. The orchestral harp is very big and often beautifully decorated. It has 48 strings which stretch from the wavy top edge of the instrument to the wide, sloping side. Harpists tilt the harp toward them as they play.

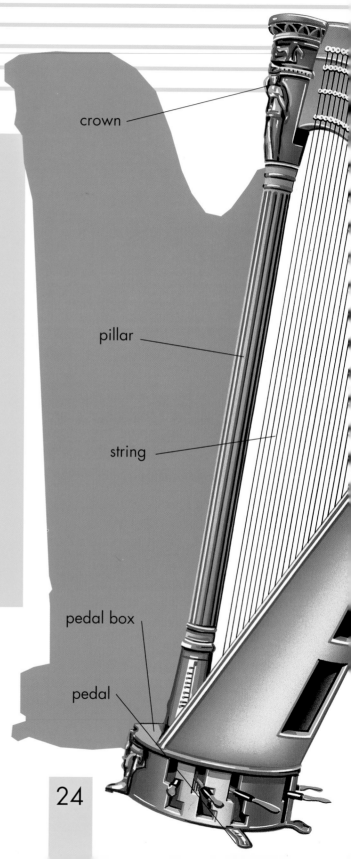

crown

pillar

string

pedal box

pedal

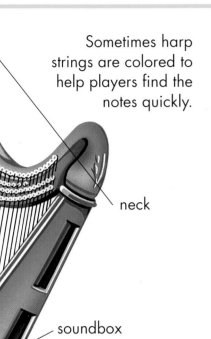

Sometimes harp strings are colored to help players find the notes quickly.

neck

soundbox

Harpists pluck the strings from both sides. Usually harpists use the right hand to play the higher (shorter) strings and the left hand to play the lower (longer) strings. Players sometimes brush their fingers across the strings to make a beautiful wave of sound. At the base of the harp there are seven pedals. Pressing the pedals makes the strings sound different notes.

Bouzouki

The bouzouki (buh-zoo-ki) is a folk instrument from Greece. The instrument has a very long neck. The eight metal strings are divided into sets of two. Each set of strings plays the same note, and the strings are always played two at a time, in their sets. The bouzouki has metal frets like the guitar.

tuning peg

fret

fingerboard

body

sound hole

bridge

string

Bouzouki players use a plectrum to pluck the metal strings.

26

Balalaika

The Russian balalaika (bal-al-eye-ka) has a body shaped like a triangle and has a flat back. The balalaika has three strings. The highest string is made of metal. Musicians pluck it with their forefinger to play the tune. The other strings are made of nylon. Players pluck them with their thumb to accompany the tune.

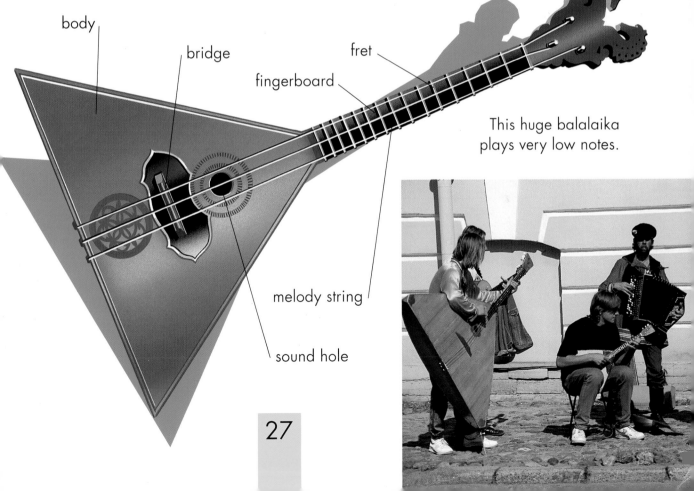

body

bridge

fret

fingerboard

This huge balalaika plays very low notes.

melody string

sound hole

27

Zither

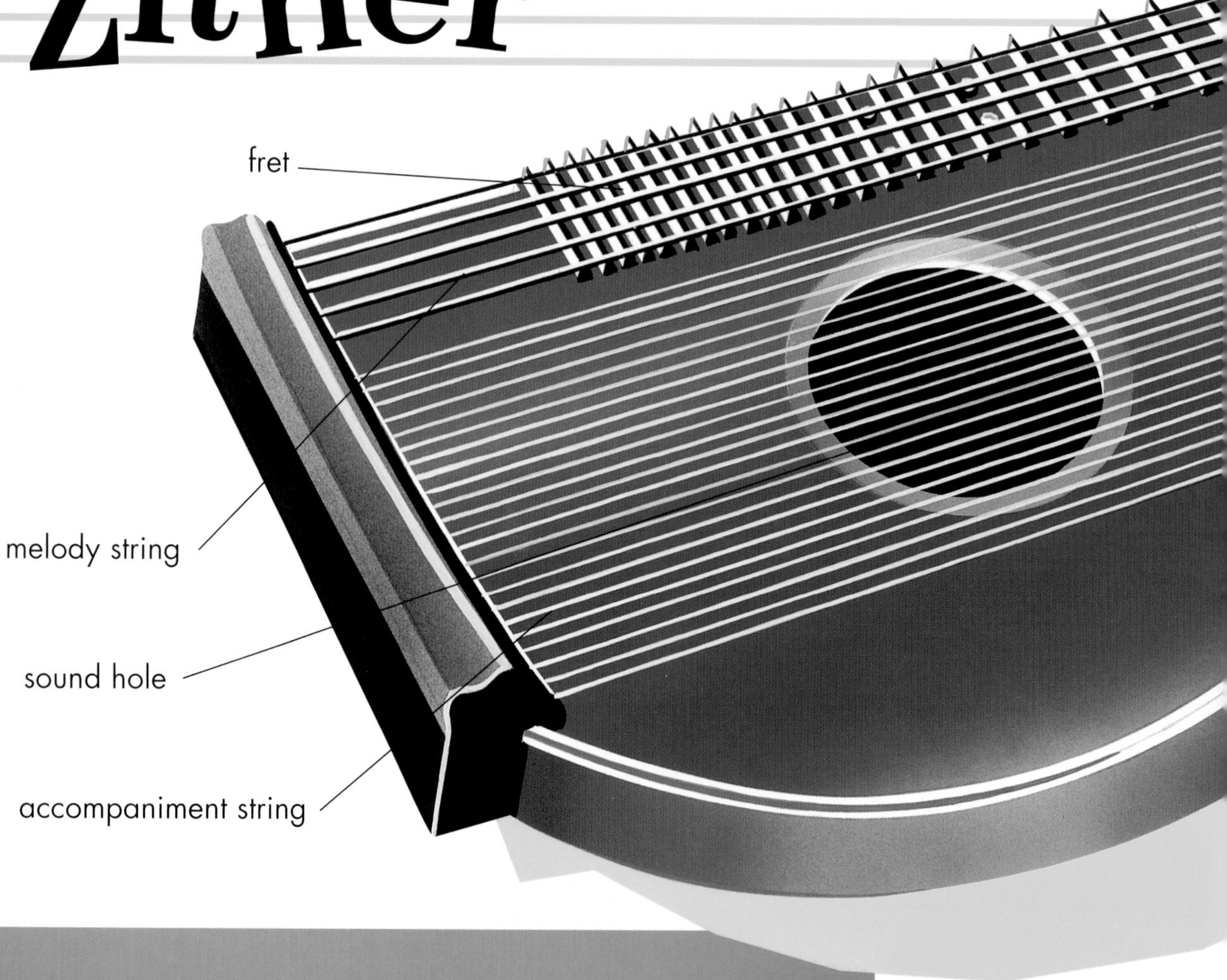

fret

melody string

sound hole

accompaniment string

The zither comes in many shapes and sizes. It is played on a table or on the player's lap. The five strings on the straight side are used to play the tune. The other strings are used to accompany it.

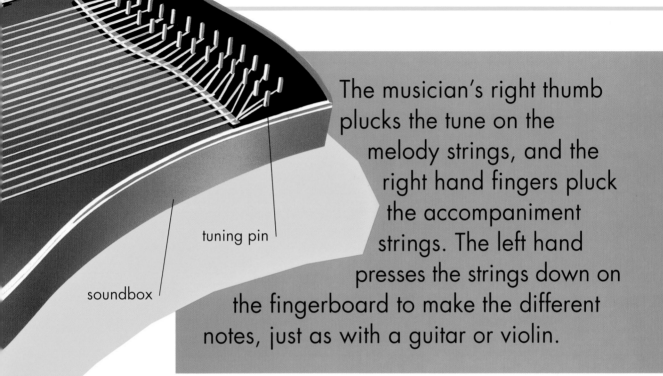

soundbox

tuning pin

The musician's right thumb plucks the tune on the melody strings, and the right hand fingers pluck the accompaniment strings. The left hand presses the strings down on the fingerboard to make the different notes, just as with a guitar or violin.

Sometimes players shake their left hand as they press down on the strings. This action makes a wavering sound in the music called vibrato.

29

Words to

accompaniment Notes that are played along with the tune.

accompany To play music alongside a singer or another player who has the tune.

adjuster A small metal grip that helps to tighten the strings on the violin, viola, cello, and double bass.

beaters Sticks of wood or wire used to hit or strike some instruments.

belly The front part of the body of a stringed instrument.

bow A long piece of wood with horsehair or nylon stretched between the ends. Musicians pull the bow across the strings.

bridge A small piece of wood or other material used to hold the strings away from the body of the instrument so that it sounds freely.

chords Groups of notes played together.

concert When players or singers perform in front of an audience.

family (of instruments) Instruments that are similar to each other.

fingerboard A long strip of wood glued to the neck of a stringed instrument. The player presses the strings against the fingerboard to make different notes.

folk music Popular tunes so old that no one knows who wrote them.

frets Thin strips, usually made of metal, on a fingerboard. They show players where to put their fingers to make notes on an instrument.

jazz A kind of pop music. In jazz, musicians often make up the music as they play it.

remember

melody A tune or song.

musician Someone who plays an instrument or sings.

neck The long end-part of a stringed instrument. The right-handed player holds the instrument by the neck with the left hand.

orchestra A large group of musicians playing together.

pedal Any part of an instrument worked by the player's foot.

performer Someone who plays or sings to other people.

plectrum A small piece of plastic or wood used to pluck some stringed instruments.

pluck To play an instrument by quickly pulling and letting go of the strings.

solo A piece of music played or sung by one performer.

soundbox The hollow body of a stringed instrument. The soundbox helps to make the instrument louder.

sound hole A round or long hole or holes cut into the belly of a stringed instrument to make it sound better.

strum To pull the fingers across the strings quickly, like a guitarist.

tuning pegs Pegs that can be turned to tighten or loosen the strings until they sound the right note.

vibrate To move up and down very quickly. When a string is bowed or plucked it vibrates.

vibrato A wavering sound in the music made by players shaking their hand as they press down on a string.

Index